ARMY RANGERS

SPECIAL FORCES: PROTECTING, BUILDING, TEACHING, AND FIGHTING

ARMY RANGERS

by Gabrielle Vanderhoof and C.F. Earl

Mason Crest Publishers

MASON CREST PUBLISHERS INC.
370 Reed Road
Broomall, Pennsylvania 19008
(866)MCP-BOOK (toll free)
www.masoncrest.com

First Printing
9 8 7 6 5 4 3 2 1

ISBN 978-1-4222-1838-9
ISBN (series) 978-1-4222-1836-5

Library of Congress Cataloging-in-Publication Data

Vanderhoof, Gabrielle.
 Army Rangers / by Gabrielle Vanderhoof and C. F. Earl.
    p. cm.
 Includes bibliographical references and index.
 1. United States. Army—Commando troops—Juvenile literature. I. Flath, Camden, 1987- II. Title.
 UA34.R36V36 2011
 356'.1670973—dc22
                        2010023795

Produced by Harding House Publishing Service, Inc.
www.hardinghousepages.com
Interior design by MK Bassett-Harvey.
Cover design by Torque Advertising Design.
Printed in USA.

With thanks and appreciation to the U.S. Military for the use of information, text, and images.

Contents

Introduction

lite forces are the tip of Freedom's spear. These small, special units are universally the first to engage, whether on reconnaissance missions into denied territory for larger conventional forces or in direct action, surgical operations, preemptive strikes, retaliatory action, and hostage rescues. They lead the way in today's war on terrorism, the war on drugs, the war on transnational unrest, and in humanitarian operations as well as nation building. When large-scale warfare erupts, they offer theater commanders a wide variety of unique, unconventional options.

Most such units are regionally oriented, acclimated to the culture and conversant in the languages of the areas where they operate. Since they deploy to those areas regularly, often for combined training exercises with indigenous forces, these elite units also serve as peacetime "global scouts," and "diplomacy multipliers," beacons of hope for the democratic aspirations of oppressed peoples all over the globe.

Elite forces are truly "quiet professionals": their actions speak louder than words. They are self-motivated, self-confidant, versatile, seasoned, mature individuals who rely on teamwork more than daring-do. Unfortunately, theirs is dangerous work. Since the 1980 attempt to rescue hostages from the U.S. embassy in Tehran, American special operations forces have suffered casualties in real-world operations at close to fifteen times the rate of U.S. conventional forces. By the very nature of the challenges that face special operations forces, training for these elite units has proven even more hazardous.

Thus it's with special pride that I join you in saluting the brave men who volunteer to serve in and support these magnificent units and who face such difficult challenges ahead.

—*Colonel John T. Carney, Jr., USAF–Ret.*
President, Special Operations Warrior Foundation

CHAPTER 1

CHAPTER 1
The History of the United States Army

ince it was first formed in 1775, the U.S. Army has served with distinction in wars all around the world. Because it can be called to serve anywhere, its soldiers have become experts in combat in a variety of scenarios, environments, and weather conditions.

Looking back into history, the U.S. Army began as a force called the Continental Army in the late eighteenth century. The United States at that time was facing the turmoil of revolution. The British rulers had placed harsh laws upon the American colonies, and a group of American leaders gathered to work out how they would achieve independence.

On June 14, 1775, at a meeting called the Second Continental Congress, the Continental Army was formed under the command of George Washington, who would go on to be America's first Commander in Chief. It was this army that fought to **repel** the British during the Revolutionary War between 1775 and 1783. The Continental Army was originally only 960 men strong. Yet it would be the seed from which the modern U.S. Army would grow.

Following the war, the Continental Army was disbanded. Now that independence was achieved, the United States Army replaced it. The President was the power behind the Army, the Commander in Chief of all the armed forces serving the United States. As Commander in Chief, the President could order the Army into battle whenever he felt military force was necessary. The country, however, could not afford to keep a large standing military at all times during the early days of both the Army and the nation. The U.S. Army grew or shrank in size depending on whether or not the country was at war.

Over the next century, the United States Army would be tested in all manner of combat situations. In the War of 1812, the Army was once again fighting the British, as well as Native American tribes funded and equipped by the British Empire. Between 1846 and 1848, U.S. Army soldiers were fighting in Mexico. But the biggest leap for the U.S. Army happened between 1861 and 1865, during the American Civil War. The U.S. Army expanded during the four years of the Civil War to become a massive fighting force of around one million men.

UNDERSTAND THE FULL MEANING

repel: To fight off and prevent the advance of an enemy force.

The Battle of Chickamauga had the second highest number of casualties in the United States Civil War (following Gettysburg).

Over the next fifty years, the U.S. Army went through many changes in size and organization. In 1917, it entered World War I. Europe had been locked in bloody battle for nearly three years, and Britain, France, and their **allies** were almost exhausted. The United States arrived in battle as one of the best trained and prepared armies in the world at that time. It had over three and a half million men in its ranks, and some of the most advanced military equipment available. During the First World War, the Army fought hard, losing thousands of men before 1918, when the war finally ended in German defeat and victory for America and its European allies.

Yet the biggest test of all for the U.S. Army came in 1941. World War II had been raging across Europe since 1939; then, in 1941, the Japanese bombed the U.S. fleet stationed at Pearl Harbor in Hawaii. The United States was now in the war. Millions of men across the United States were called up to serve in the Army, and it grew to over eight million men. These men served across the globe—in Japan and the Pacific, Africa, and Europe. They fought huge battles with German and Japanese forces. Experienced German units were amazed at how quickly U.S. recruits became hard fighting soldiers, and the U.S. Contribution to the war meant that victory for the Allies was certain. Both Germany and Japan surrendered in 1945, after the Allies stormed Berlin, and the United States dropped two atomic bombs on Japanese cities, Hiroshima and Nagasaki. During World War II, the U.S.

UNDERSTAND THE FULL MEANING

allies: Those fighting on the same side in a military conflict.

Army was also reorganized into different parts, with each part called a Command: Army Ground Forces, Army Air Forces (the Air Force would be come separate in 1947), and Army Service Forces. The Women's Army Corps was also formed in 1942.

This image shows 1st Battalion Army Rangers at dawn on November 8, 1942, at a French coastal gun position that they captured during a night of fighting, probably at Arzew, Algeria.

World War II showed what a remarkable fighting force the U.S. Army had become since its birth before the Revolutionary War. Since 1945, it has continued to prove this in many conflicts around the world. Between 1950 and 1953, the Army was engaged in the Korean War, fighting **communist** North Korean forces invading the South. Starting

United States Army infantrymen fighting in the Korean War.

in 1955, U.S. Army soldiers also fought communist forces in the Vietnam War, combating the **guerrilla** tactics of the Viet Cong. American Army soldiers also fought in Operation Desert Storm, driving invading Iraqi Army forces from Kuwait. Throughout the 1990s the U.S. Army was involved in a variety of peacekeeping missions around the world. And since the terrorist attacks of September 11, 2001, the Army has been involved in both the wars in Afghanistan and Iraq.

Today, the Army is one of the three military departments that report to the United States Department of Defense, along with the Navy and Air Force. More than one million Americans are serving in today's Army, Army National Guard, and Army Reserves. The Army requested more than $140 billion for its 2009 budget, making it one of the largest military organizations in history.

The Army's mission is "to fight and win the Nation's wars by providing prompt, **sustained** land **dominance** across the full range of military operations and **spectrum** of conflict in support of combatant commanders." In general,

UNDERSTAND THE FULL MEANING

communist: A government that closely controls the economic freedom, and often other rights, of its citizens.

guerrilla: A style of warfare in which smaller forces use tactics like raids and ambushes against a larger army.

sustained: Something that is stable over a relatively long period of time.

dominance: The state of being in control.

spectrum: A wide range of variable conditions.

the Army is responsible for protecting the United States of America and its global interests, be they policy-oriented or **strategic** in nature. Primarily on land, the Army is capable of waging war and keeping the peace, all the while remaining ready for any military scenario.

U.S. soldiers speak to residents during a walk-and-talk through a market in Nassir Wa Salaam, Iraq. During the walk-through, the soldiers spoke to merchants about market access problems and distributed micro-grant packets for economic development aid.

The Army is made up of two distinct and equally important components: the active components, the Army National Guard; and the reserve components, the United States Army Reserve. Regardless of which component, the Army conducts two types of missions: operational and institutional. The operational army consists of numbered armies, corps, divisions, brigades, and battalions that conduct full-spectrum operations all around the world. The institutional Army supports the operational Army by providing the **infrastructure** necessary to raise, train, equip, **deploy**, and ensure the readiness of all Army forces; it also allows the Army to expand rapidly in time of war. Without the institutional Army, the operational Army cannot function; without the operational Army, the institutional Army has no purpose.

In the twenty-first century, the men and women of the modern United States Army work tirelessly to combat threats to American national security. Serving in the wars in Iraq and Afghanistan, as well as in a **humanitarian** capacity around the world (most recently after the earthquakes in Haiti in January 2010), the U.S. Army is one of the strongest, best-trained, and effective military units the world has ever known.

UNDERSTAND THE FULL MEANING

strategic: Something that is planned out for a specific goal.

infrastructure: Those systems within an organization that are basic to its operation.

deploy: To move military forces into an area of conflict.

humanitarian: Those actions with the goal of bringing aid and assistance to a civilian population.

CHAPTER 2

Overview of the Army Rangers

The United States Army Rangers are among the best light-infantry in the U.S. Army. The Rangers are responsible for planning and carrying out special operations missions that support the international policy and strategic aims of the United States. These soldiers are regularly involved in combat and are highly trained to deal with the stresses combat presents. Rangers are sent on missions of extraordinary danger, often in enemy-occupied territory. Day or night, in all conditions, across all kinds of terrain, the Rangers are employed to strike quickly and effectively against enemy targets, usually with **lethal** force.

UNDERSTAND THE FULL MEANING

lethal: A force that is deadly.

In order to remain ready for deployment at any time, the Rangers must train all the time. Today's Rangers train in arctic, jungle, desert, and mountain environments so that they can operate under any conditions. The philosophy that forms the foundation of the training techniques used by the Army Rangers allows them to maintain constant readiness. During training, Rangers are held to the highest physical and mental standards, completing live-fire exercises designed to feel as real as possible. Rangers train in all kinds of weather and types of terrain, day and night, to help prepare them for any situation. In the course of their training, Ranger **candidates** must complete a challenging selection program, facing physical and mental challenges that only the Army's most elite soldiers are able to endure. More than anything, the Army teaches Rangers to expect the unexpected.

HISTORY OF THE ARMY RANGERS

Rangers have fought in almost every American conflict, from the American Revolution to the Civil War to Vietnam. They liberated American POWs in Japan in World War II and fended off British attacks on the United States in the War of 1812. In some form, whether as a trained volunteer force or as a trained military unit, Rangers have always heeded the call of duty at key moments in American history.

UNDERSTAND THE FULL MEANING

candidates: Are people being considered for a particular job or program.

RANGERS IN THE EIGHTEENTH CENTURY

The history of the Army Rangers dates to before the American Revolutionary War, when Captain Benjamin Church and Major Robert Rogers organized Ranger units in order to fight during the French-Indian War in the mid 1700s. Major Rogers is best known today for writing the nineteen standing orders that still act as a centerpiece of today's twenty-first-century Ranger training.

The French and Indian War was fought between France and Britain in North America from 1754–1763. During the war, Major Robert Rogers raised and commanded the famous Rogers' Rangers, a forerunner of today's Army Rangers.

Roger's Rangers Standing Orders:

1. Don't forget nothing.

2. Have your musket clean as a whistle, hatchet scoured, sixty rounds powder and ball, and be ready to march at a minutes warning.

3. When you're on the march, act the way you would if you was sneaking up on a deer. See enemy first.

4. Tell the truth about what you see and what you do. There is an army depending on us for correct information. You can lie all you please when you tell other folks about the Rangers, but don't ever lie to a Ranger or an officer.

5. Don't ever take a chance you don't have to.

6. When you're on the march, we march as a single file, far enough apart so one shot can't go thru two men.

7. If we strike swamps, or soft ground, we spread out abreast, so it's hard to track us.

8. When we march, we keep moving till dark, so as to give the enemy the least chance at us.

9. When we camp, half the party stays awake while the other half sleeps.

10. If we take prisoners, we keep 'em separate till we have had time to examine them, lest they cook up a story between 'em.

11. Don't ever march the same way. Take a different route so you won't be ambushed.

12. No matter whether we travel in big parties or little ones, each party has to keep a scout 20 yards ahead, 20 yards on each flank and 20 yards in the rear, so the main body can't be surprised and wiped out.

13. Every night you'll be told where to meet if surrounded by a superior force.

14. Don't sit down to eat without posting sentries.

15. Don't sleep beyond dawn, Dawn's when the French and Indians attack.

16. Don't cross a river by a regular ford.

17. If somebody's trailing you, make a circle, come back onto your own tracks, and ambush the folks that aim to ambush you.

18. Don't stand up when the enemy's coming against you. Kneel down, lie down, or hide behind a tree.

19. Let the enemy come till he's almost close enough to touch. Then let him have it and jump out and finish him with your hatchet.

In 1775, the Continental Congress organized eight companies of top riflemen in order to combat the British in the Revolutionary War. Two years later, commanded by Dan Morgan, these soldiers, most of them frontiersmen, came to be known as the Corps of Rangers. Elsewhere during the war, Francis Marion—known as "the Swamp Fox"—organized another group of Rangers to fight the British. His soldiers were called Marion's Partisans.

During the American Revolutionary War, Francis Marion, "The Swamp Fox," formed a group of rangers. Today, Marion is considered one of the fathers of modern guerrilla warfare, and is credited in the lineage of the United States Army Rangers.

In the War of 1812, frontier settlers were trained to become Rangers and serve alongside the rest of the army. These soldiers fought off British and Native American attacks in what was then called the Northwest Territory. By boat and on horseback, the Rangers patrolled the regions of modern Ohio and Illinois.

During the Civil War, Rangers were also active in the United States, the most famous of them fighting to break from the Union in the Confederate Army. John Singleton Mosby, for example, was likely the most famous Confederate Ranger at the time of the Civil War. Mosby's Rangers' raids on Union Army bases and camps were so successful that the territory his men occupied was known as Mosby's Confederacy. The only Union units to successfully mount counterattacks on Mosby's men were Ranger units as well, the most well known the Loudoun Rangers, hailing from what is now Loudoun County, Virginia.

RANGERS IN WORLD WAR II

Almost a century later, during America's involvement in World War II, the Army organized and activated six Ranger battalions for deployment in North Africa, Europe, and Japan. The Army looked to British Commandos as the model for these Ranger battalions.

Major William Darby activated the First Ranger Battalion on June 19, 1942. Each of the soldiers in this battalion were handpicked volunteers, some of whom had seen combat in the famous, though failed, Dieppe Raid, and they had trained with both British and Canadian commando units. Started by Darby in Northern Ireland, the First Battalion fought initially in the North African theater in World War II, landing in Algeria. They worked to prevent the Nazi invasion of Europe by taking the port at Arzew and then fought in the Tunisian Battles.

Colonel Darby (who had risen in rank since his time with the First Ranger Battalion) also trained and activated the Third and Fourth Ranger Battalions while he was in Africa engaged in the Tunisian campaign. In fact, to begin with, soldiers from the First Battalion made up the Third and Fourth Ranger Battalions, after Darby divided the First into thirds so that the Rangers could better serve the Allied war effort in Europe. Taken together, Darby's First, Third, and Fourth Ranger Battalions were known as the Ranger Force. Together, the Ranger Force led the Allied invasion of Sicily, and then played a key role in the Allied landing at Anzio, one of the first operations of the Allied offensive into Italy. The First Battalion fought Mussolini's Facist forces in Sicily and Italy as part of the Ranger Force, then Hitler's Nazis in occupied Europe, and finally the battalion served in India-Burma before being awarded the Presidential Unit Citation. The Ranger Force was the first to wear the scroll insignia worn by today's Ranger battalions.

UNDERSTAND THE FULL MEANING

commando: Is a soldier, or unit of soldiers, that uses specialized tactics against military targets.

theater: A geographical region within a larger-scale military conflict.

The Second and Fifth Ranger Battalion stormed the beaches of Normandy as part of the Allied invasion of Nazi-occupied France. On June 6, 1944, the Allied forces landed in Northern France from the United Kingdom. At a number of beach landing points—code named Utah, Omaha, Gold, Juno, and Sword—Canadian, British, and American forces

Army Rangers by the ladders they used to scale the cliffs of Omaha Beach on "D-Day," June 6, 1944.

fought, all the while being fired upon by German soldiers on the cliffs above. The Second and Fifth Battalions landed at Omaha Beach.

During the fighting in Normandy, Brigadier General Norman D. Cota, serving as Assistant Division Commander of the Twenty-Ninth Infantry Division, ordered his men to advance up the beach, engaging German soldiers as they went, until they had cleared the beach enough for Allied forces to move inland. His orders to Lieutenant Colonel Max Schneider, leader of the Fifth Ranger Battalion, were simple, but they remain at the core of what it means to be a U.S. Army Ranger. "Rangers, lead the way!" he yelled. This is the motto of the Rangers to this day.

The Fifth Battalion scaled the cliffs over Omaha Beach, eliminating the threat of German gunners focusing their fire on American soldiers moving up the beach. Companies D, E, and F of the Second Ranger Battalion, acting alongside the 116th Infantry Regiment, Twenty-Ninth Infantry Division, captured additional gun **emplacements** above Omaha after fighting through a heavily fortified German force. Under machine gun fire and **mortar** attack, Rangers climbed rope ladders up the cliffs of Pointe Du Hoc, taking the lead at a vital point in American military history.

UNDERSTAND THE FULL MEANING

emplacements: Prepared positions for the placement of large-scale weapons.

mortar: A front-loading cannon designed to fire at a high angle.

reconnaissance: A mission to obtain information about the activities and resources of an enemy.

The Sixth Ranger Battalion was the only one of the six to operate in the Pacific theater during the Second World War. The majority of the missions carried out by the Sixth Battalion involved **reconnaissance** or combat patrols behind enemy lines. In January of 1945, the Sixth Battalion liberated American Prisoners of War from a Japanese POW camp located at Cabanatuan in the Philippines. The liberation of the American POWs involved a 24-mile infiltration behind enemy lines. Though the Japanese soldiers outnumbered the American forces by almost two-to-one, the Rangers managed to rescue more than 500 captured Americans and kill more than 200 enemy soldiers. During the mission, two Rangers were killed, while ten were wounded.

In 1943, the Seventy-Fifth Infantry Regiment, what would later become the Seventy-Fifth Ranger Regiment, was activated for the first time. Serving in China, Burma, and India during World War II, the Seventy-Fifth Regiment came to be known as Merrill's Marauders, named for its commander, Major General Frank Merrill.

At the end of World War II, the U.S. Army deactivated the Ranger Battalions that had been operating during the war.

THE KOREAN AND VIETNAM WARS

In 1950, at the outset of the Korean War, the Rangers were called upon once again. In all, fifteen Ranger Companies were organized and activated during the war. The Rangers served alongside several different regiments during their deployment. They conducted scouting, raid, ambush, assault, and counterattack missions—what was called "out front" work.

An army infantryman is shown moving through the jungle about 40 miles east of Saigon, Vietnam.

Rangers also served in the Vietnam War. On the first of January, 1969, the Seventy-Fifth Infantry (what would later become today's Seventy-Fifth Ranger Regiment) was reorganized, fifteen Ranger companies being activated in the process. Thirteen of these companies served in Vietnam itself, until they were disbanded on August 15, 1972.

In 1974, the Army Chief of Staff, General Creighton Abrams, ordered that a Ranger Battalion be organized and activated. The First Ranger Battalion, initially part of the Seventy-Fifth Infantry (later the Seventy-Fifth Ranger Regiment) was activated on July 1, 1974. A few months later, in October of the same year, the Army activated the Second Ranger Battalion. These modern Ranger Battalions were called to action in 1980, when parts of the First Battalion, still part of the Seventy-Fifth Infantry, participated in the attempted rescue of Americans during the Iranian hostage crisis. The Third Ranger Battalion would be activated a few years later, in 1984.

It was not until February of 1986 that the Seventy-Fifth Ranger Regiment was officially designated as such. The modern Army Rangers have served proudly in the Seventy-Fifth Regiment ever since.

In the 1990s, the Seventy-Fifth Regiment was deployed in service to a variety of engagements, including Operation Desert Storm and United Nations operations in Somalia. Between February and April of 1991, elements of the First Ranger Battalion were deployed to Saudi Arabia, where they supported troops in Operation Desert Storm, protecting America's allies from Saddam Hussein's invasion of Kuwait.

In 1993, parts of the Third Ranger Battalion deployed to Somalia to help U.N. peacekeepers stabilize the war-ravaged nation, its population on the verge of starvation. In a daytime raid in October of the same year, Rangers fought off the attacking forces of a Somali warlord for eighteen hours straight, killing more than 600 enemy troops with the assistance of civilian fighters and U.N. troops. Many have called this combat the fiercest and bloodiest since the Vietnam War. Called the Battle of Mogadishu, the events of October 3 and 4, 1993, are the basis for the movie *Black Hawk Down*.

A U.S. helicopter as it flies over a Mogadishu residential area in December of 1992 at the beginning of Operation Restore Hope, the humanitarian operation in Somalia from December 5, 1992–May 4, 1993.

TODAY'S RANGERS: THE SEVENTY-FIFTH RANGER REGIMENT

The modern Army Rangers are all part of the Seventy-Fifth Ranger Regiment, a deadly, adaptable, and highly skilled military force. Today's Rangers are trained to execute special operations in support of United States policy and strategic goals. The Seventy-Fifth Ranger Regiment is made up of three battalions of infantry and one battalion of support troops. Each of these four battalions is able to deploy to any part of the globe in mere hours. Rangers are physically and mentally prepared for combat operations at all times.

The Rangers are able to perform a variety of missions and military actions, including (but not limited to):

- Infiltrating and exfiltrating (that is, getting in and out of) the most dangerous regions of the world by sea, air, and land.

- Carrying out raids on enemy bases, camps, or strategic objectives.

- Rescue of captured American military personnel from the nation's enemies.

- Recovery of equipment lost or taken in the field.

- Attacking key enemy targets, whether to disable a key enemy capability or to capture or kill enemy personnel.

- Seizing, destroying, or defending vital strategic facilities, such as airfields.

No matter the number of Rangers involved in any given operation, the unit is able to fulfill all these responsibilities at all times. In order to be prepared to take on these challenges, the Seventy-Fifth Ranger Regiment keeps its soldiers to the highest of standards during their selection and training, with a particular emphasis on realistic combat training. All Rangers are highly trained, skilled, and prepared at all times. The Seventy-Fifth Ranger Regiment proudly serves the U.S. Army, defending American interests abroad.

BATTALIONS OF THE SEVENTY-FIFTH RANGER REGIMENT

The three main Ranger Battalions are made up of 660 soldiers. These battalions are divided into three rifle companies and one headquarters company (which coordinates and directs operations). The Ranger Battalions that make up the Seventy-Fifth Ranger Regiment are always prepared to deploy anywhere in the world with just 18 hours notice ahead of time.

First Battalion

The First Battalion was initially created to be part of the Seventy-Fifth Infantry, activated on January 31, 1974. General Creighton Abrams recognized the need for an expert military force that could quickly react to any situation and so ordered the activation of the modern Rangers. From March through June of 1974, selection of the soldiers who would become the first Rangers in the Army since Vietnam continued at Fort Benning, where the unit was to be trained. The First Battalion was stationed at Fort Stewart in Georgia before being stationed at the Hunter Army Airfield (also in Georgia), in 1978.

In 1980, the preparation and training that the First Battalion had completed before their attempted rescue of the hostages in the Iranian hostage crisis laid the foundation for today's special operations capabilities. It was during this time that the modern Rangers (as well as other American Special Operations units) solidified their training requirements, their operational **tactics**, and the equipment they would use on missions. The Rangers were viewed as so effective in combat at the time, that the First Battalion was deployed to Grenada in 1983 on a mission to rescue American citizens and stabilize the democratic government in that country.

Before 1986, Ranger battalions served as part of the Seventy-Fifth Infantry, but that changed when the Seventy-Fifth Infantry became the Seventy-Fifth Ranger Regiment in March of that year. From that time forward, all Rangers served in the Seventy-Fifth Ranger Regiment, including the First Battalion.

At the end of 1989, the First Ranger Battalion saw combat again in support of Operation Just Cause in Panama, specifically, in their capture of Tocumen Airfield, a key strategic objective for the United States, and the missions they conducted throughout the operation.

Only a few years later, in 1991, members of the First Battalion deployed to Saudi Arabia, where they took part in

UNDERSTAND THE FULL MEANING

tactics: Methods and strategies used in warfare.

missions supporting Operation Desert Storm. In cooperation with America's allies in that conflict, the Rangers conducted raid missions from February to April of 1991, many of which were key to the success of the U.S. operation.

Second Battalion

Serving as part of the Seventy-Fifth Infantry at that time, the Second Ranger Battalion was officially effective starting on October 1, 1974. In the early months of 1975, the leadership of the modern Rangers was trained at Fort Benning. They then worked to pass on the values of the Army Rangers to the first generation of Second Battalion Rangers. By April, the first training exercises of the Second Battalion were begun in full. Starting with small-team training and moving toward company training, the Second Ranger Battalion instilled into each soldier the expertise and knowledge the Rangers embody. In 1975, the Army declared that the Second Battalion was able to deploy to any part of the world, ready for combat. This intense training was a precursor to 1980, when the modern Ranger era truly began with a revision of Special Operations tactics.

During Operation Urgent Fury in Grenada (conducted in 1983), the First and Second Ranger Battalions parachuted into Point Salinas Airbase. They were given the tasks of rescuing American citizens from a medical university in Grenada, and at the same time, reestablishing democratic rule in the island nation. After landing in the country, the two Ranger Battalions conducted a variety of missions intended to eliminate resistance to American forces.

An Army Ranger from the 1st Battalion, 75th Ranger Regiment patrol the streets of a mock city during a training exercise conducted at Fort Bragg, North Carolina.

In 1989, the entire Seventy-Fifth Ranger Regiment was deployed to Panama in support of Operation Just Cause. All three Ranger Battalions served a key role in the success of the U.S. operation, including the American assault on General Manuel Noriega's beach house and the defeat of major elements of the Panamanian Defense Force.

In 1994, the Second Battalion deployed to Haiti to serve as part of Operation Uphold Democracy. Two years later, the battalion would distinguish itself while training in Panama, where it stopped a riot inside a refugee camp in 1996, during Operation Safe Haven.

THIRD BATTALION

After Operation Urgent Fury, conducted in Grenada, the Army ordered the activation of the Third Ranger Battalion. In April 1984, Fort Benning began the selection process for the new battalion. In October of the same year, the Third Battalion was activated, making it the largest U.S. Army Ranger force since the days of World War II.

In 1989, the Third Battalion assisted in Operation Just Cause in Panama. It aided the First Battalion in its capture of the Tocumen Airfield, and it also spearheaded the seizure of the Rio Hato Airfield. The Third Battalion assisted the U.S. victory in Panama.

In 1993, Rangers from the Third Battalion were deployed to Somalia to assist the United Nations operations in that country. In October of that year, a few months after the Rangers first landed in Somalia and nine years since the activation of the Third Battalion, members of the unit conducted a daytime raid in Mogadishu that resulted in the most intense combat U.S. soldiers had seen since the Vietnam War. The Battle of Mogadishu, as it came to be called, was vicious and bloody. Nineteen Rangers lost their lives, though the losses the Rangers sustained were slight compared to the more than 600 enemy fighters they killed between the 3rd and 4th of October. In 2001, members of the Third Battalion deployed to Somalia again, this time to appear in the film *Black Hawk Down* in order to honor the Rangers lost during the battle.

REGIMENTAL SPECIAL TROOPS BATTALION (RSTB)

The Regimental Special Troops Battalion (RSTB) assists the Seventy-Fifth Ranger Regiment and other Special Operations Forces by providing communications, technology, and **intelligence** in order to support the Rangers in the field. The RSTB are also able to assist other military task forces, if the need arises. The Regimental Special Troops Battalion is the newest of the Seventy-Fifth Regiment's Ranger Battalions, activated in 2006 after the Rangers' prolonged deployment in Iraq and Afghanistan necessitated additional reconnaissance and technological support.

DAILY LIFE FOR THE ARMY RANGERS

Rangers live much the same way most Army units do. During a typical round of duty, Rangers will have their nights

UNDERSTAND THE FULL MEANING

intelligence: Information about the activities of an enemy force.

and weekends to themselves. Each year, Rangers receive thirty days of vacation, called leave. During their service and training, Rangers may also have federal holidays off or sometimes the same holiday long weekends that civilians enjoy. Each Ranger is also able to take advantage of the opportunity to attend one of many military (and some civilian schools) that coincide with his Military Occupational Specialty (MOS).

Each Ranger must participate in several large-scale training exercises that take place both within the United States and overseas. So that Rangers may plan their personal lives around these required events, the Army plans training of this sort a year in advance, informing the Rangers as to when they must attend training.

Unmarried Rangers live in barracks that resemble dormitories, while married Rangers live either in quarters that can support a family or in the community surrounding the base at which they are stationed. The families of Rangers are able to attend several unit functions throughout the year and are also kept informed about deployments and training events that may keep Rangers away from home. The Seventy-Fifth Ranger Regiment prides itself on being one of the top Family Readiness Groups in the U.S. Army. These groups provide spouses and families with support and are run by the Army, bringing families closer to each other and to the experience of their loved ones serving as Rangers through communication between families and the chain of command, clubs, activities, and other support networks.

The Ranger Creed

Recognizing that I volunteered as a Ranger, fully knowing the hazards of my chosen profession, I will always endeavor to uphold the prestige, honor, and high esprit de corps of my Ranger Regiment.

Acknowledging the fact that a Ranger is a more elite soldier who arrives at the cutting edge of battle by land, sea, or air, I accept the fact that as a Ranger my country expects me to move further, faster and fight harder than any other soldier.

Never shall I fail my comrades. I will always keep myself mentally alert, physically strong, and morally straight; I will shoulder more than my share of the task whatever it may be, one hundred percent and then some.

Gallantly will I show the world that I am a specially selected and well-trained soldier. My courtesy to superior officers, neatness of dress, and care of equipment shall set the example for others to follow.

Energetically will I meet the enemies of my country. I shall defeat them on the field of battle for I am better trained and will fight with all my might. Surrender is not a Ranger word. I will never leave a fallen comrade to fall into the hands of the enemy, and under no circumstances will I ever embarrass my country.

Readily will I display the intestinal fortitude required to fight on to the Ranger objective and complete the mission, though I be the lone survivor.

CHAPTER 3
Ranger Training

In order for a civilian to become a U.S. Army Ranger, they must complete many different phases of training across several different schools, operating from different bases. From Basic Combat Training through Ranger School, the training to become a Ranger is physically and mentally demanding, pushing soldiers to their limits.

BASIC COMBAT TRAINING

Basic Combat Training prepares civilian recruits for service in the Army. Also known as BCT, Basic Training takes nine weeks. Over the course of that time, recruits learn how to work with other soldiers, carry out their duties in high-stress situations, and employ the tactics used by the U.S. Military.

In order to graduate from Basic Training, recruits must also achieve and maintain a level of physical fitness that allows them to serve effectively. Basic Combat Training consists of three main phases.

The Seven Core Army Values

In Basic Combat Training, each soldier learns to live the Seven Core Army Values, values that exemplify what being a soldier means, that inform the character of every soldier in the United States Army. The Seven Core Army Values are as follows:

- loyalty
- duty
- respect
- selfless service
- honor
- integrity
- personal courage

Civilians may be familiar with these words, but soldiers must embody them, in and out of uniform.

PHASE ONE: RED PHASE

After ensuring that all recruits are physically and mentally prepared to start Basic Training (often through passage of the Army Physical Fitness Test (APFT)), the Army gives

Soldiers practice rappelling down a four-story building to enhance their skills as infantrymen.

them haircuts and uniforms, and BCT begins. In phase one of Basic Training, recruits learn about the tactics the Army uses; what the military must do in the event of a nuclear, biological, or chemical attack on the United States; and how to live the Seven Core Army Values. Recruits also learn about the history of the Army.

PHASE TWO: WHITE PHASE

In the second phase of Basic Combat Training, recruits receive weapons and tactics training. Along with other recruits, they participate in marksmanship, marching, **rappelling**, and other exercises. The Army's goal in this first phase is too begin to train civilian recruits in the skills needed for military service, but also to instill recruits with the confidence of soldiers serving the United States.

PHASE THREE: BLUE PHASE

In the third and final phase of basic training, soldiers continue to learn how to effectively use the weapons and tactics of the U.S. Army. They participate in nighttime **infiltration** exercises, go on long marches, and become experts in the use of grenades and machine guns (including some of those used by the Army Rangers). After finishing all the third phase's requirements, soldiers are ready to graduate BCT.

UNDERSTAND THE FULL MEANING

rappelling: A technique allowing for the rapid descent of a vertical surface such as a cliff or wall by sliding down a rope.

infiltration: Secretly gaining access to an enemy's position.

GRADUATION

After recruits have been pushed to their limits, families and friends can attend graduation ceremonies that celebrate the great accomplishment of enduring the grueling training to become a soldier in the U.S. Army.

Soldiers on a march during Basic Combat Training.

ADVANCED INDIVIDUAL TRAINING

After completing Basic Combat Training, recruits are given the opportunity to move to Advanced Individual Training (AIT). In this phase of their training, soldiers learn the skills they will need to effectively perform the specialized tasks required of them during their Army service. At one of a wide variety of Advanced Individual Training schools, soldiers become experts in a specific field, whether it's chemistry, engineering, communications, or combat. AIT involves hands-on training and top-quality instruction. Here are a few examples of the AIT schools soldiers have the opportunity to attend:

- *Engineering School*: Here students learn the skills that will allow them to perform a variety of engineering missions in the U.S. Army. Whether building a bridge or analyzing data, soldiers who graduate from the Engineering School are absolutely prepared for any engineering challenge.

- *Infantry School*: Soldiers become experts in the combat for which most infantryman (including the Army Rangers) must always be prepared.

- *Military Intelligence School*: Students learn to gather the information and tactical intelligence that all branches of the military, including the Army, needs in order to operate effectively.

U.S. ARMY AIRBORNE SCHOOL

The First Battalion (Airborne), 507th Infantry Regiment has the task of operating and maintaining the U.S Army Airborne School, where soldiers who have completed Basic

U.S. Army Advanced Individual Training (AIT) soldiers prepare to secure their perimeter after their convoy came under attack during the convoy operations portion of their field training exercise.

Combat Training learn to operate parachutes and complete parachute jumps in preparation for the missions they will carry out as Army Rangers. The Airborne School instructors wear black berets and are known around the world as "black hats." These instructors come from the Army, Marine Corps, Navy, and Air Force.

The First Battalion is divided into six companies. The first, Headquarters Company, is responsible for organizing the Airborne School and carrying out administration duties for the First Battalion. Four companies (A, B, C, and D Companies) provide instruction for the soldiers going through the Basic Airborne Course. Finally, E Company teaches the battalion and soldiers in BAC how to use parachute equipment and provides assistance when needed.

Students at the Airborne School receive instruction from the same sergeants and leaders throughout the three phases of training. This strategy of teaching is employed in order to maximize unit **cohesion** and decrease discipline problems.

AIRBORNE SCHOOL TRAINING

While at the U.S. Airborne School, trainees make their way through three stages of intense training, preparing for the final stage of training, in which soldiers make five training jumps from a plane more than a thousand feet in the air. The Airborne School is located at Fort Benning, Georgia.

UNDERSTAND THE FULL MEANING

cohesion: A strong feeling of unity that allows a group to work together successfully.

Training at the Airborne School lasts three weeks, one for each phase of training.

GROUND WEEK

During Ground Week, students learn the skills they'll need in order to make their first parachute jump. Students complete exercises using a variety of towers and what is called a mock door, a version of a plane door used for training. To move forward in their Airborne training, soldiers must complete jumps from test towers and pass all physical requirements for the Airborne School.

AIRBORNE TOWER WEEK

After completing Ground Week, students at Airborne School continue their training during Airborne Tower Week. In addition to honing their jump skills using towers and mock jumps, Tower Week also introduces "mass exit," which involves many soldiers jumping in an orderly way from a single plane door as efficiently as possible. In order to master this operation, students use the mock door at the top of a tower for mass-exit training exercises. During Tower Week, students must jump from 34- and 250-foot towers.

AIRBORNE JUMP WEEK

Once Airborne School students have finished both Ground and Tower Week, they are prepared to move onto Jump Week, the final phase of their Airborne training. During Jump Week, students must complete five parachute jumps from aircraft flying at 1,250 feet. Two of these jumps are called combat equipment jumps, in which students must

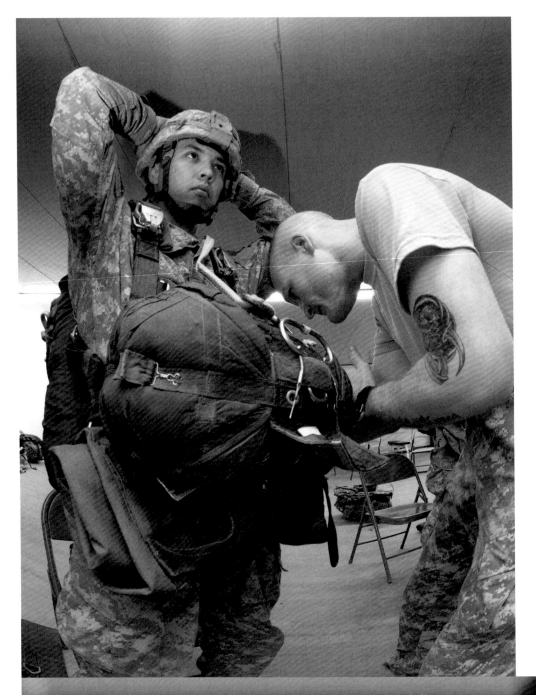

Two paratroopers practice their parachute inspection skills at Airborne School.

complete a jump successfully in full combat gear (and while carrying a fake weapon). The other three jumps are known as "Hollywood" jumps, and only require that students jump with a parachute and reserve chute. One of the five mandatory jumps is usually conducted at night, though a night jump is not mandatory if Jump Week includes a three-day federal holiday weekend and a night jump is not possible due to scheduling.

GRADUATION

The Airborne School's graduation ceremony is usually held at nine o'clock in the morning on the Friday of Jump Week. Occasionally, students may graduate immediately after finishing their final jump, right on the drop zone (DZ), should weather or other issue cause cancellation or potential delay of the normal ceremony. Family and friends of Airborne School students are permitted to come to the graduation ceremony, and even watch some of the jumps students complete from the DZ.

RANGER ASSESSMENT AND SELECTION PROGRAM

After graduating from Airborne School, soldiers who will go on to become Army Rangers are assigned to the Seventy-Fifth Ranger Regiment in order to attend the Ranger Assessment and Selection Program (also called RASP). This program begins immediately after graduation from Airborne School.

The Ranger Liaison (part of one of the training divisions of the Seventy-Fifth Ranger Regiment) will pick up Airborne School students from graduation so they may start RASP. The Ranger Assessment and Selection Program is designed to make sure that each Ranger candidate meets the standards for service in the Seventy-Fifth Ranger Regiment. The program assesses the abilities of candidates but also trains these soldiers in the skills required to become a U.S. Army Ranger.

A soldier climbs over a 20-foot rope climb obstacle during Army Ranger training.

RASP is split into two main phases for junior enlisted soldiers, who have completed Basic Combat Training, Advanced Individual Training, and then Airborne School before entering RASP. The first phase lasts for four weeks, during which time candidates are tested for physical fitness, mental endurance, and intelligence, all the while training in the combat skills for which the Rangers are known. The second phase is based around improving candidates' marksmanship, teaching them demolition expertise, and building their tactical knowledge. Officers, on the other hand, attend a program that takes three weeks to complete. In this version of RASP, officers are tested for physical and mental endurance, as well as leadership skills. Officers also learn about the kinds of Special Operations tactics used by the Seventy-Fifth Ranger Regiment.

During their training, all potential Rangers must complete:

- daily physical training
- a test of Ranger history
- the Army Physical Fitness Test (APFT)
- training in how to read maps
- extensive training in combat
- the Combat Water Survival Test
- a course in tying knots
- marches of six, eight, and ten miles
- training in both night and day navigation on land

ASSIGNMENT TO A RANGER BATTALION

After completing RASP, a soldier officially becomes a U.S. Army Ranger. He is then assigned to the Seventy-Fifth Ranger Regiment, either to one of the three active Ranger Battalions or to the Seventy-Fifth Ranger Regiment's Headquarters. The First Ranger Battalion is stationed at Hunter Army Airfield in Savannah, Georgia. The Second Battalion is located at Fort Lewis, Washington, outside Seattle. The Third Battalion is located at Fort Benning, Georgia. The Regimental Special Troops Battalion and Seventy-Fifth Ranger Regiment Headquarters are also located at Fort Benning.

ARMY RANGER SCHOOL

Though not run by or officially part of the Army Rangers, the Ranger School does train Rangers who seek to advance in their careers or further their skills and education. Ranger School prepares Ranger-qualified soldiers to become leaders within the Seventy-Fifth Ranger Regiment (all leadership positions in the Ranger Regiment require graduation from Ranger School), and non-Ranger-qualified officers to become part of the Ranger Regiment. The school is recognized as one of the top programs for producing the Army's battlefield leadership, specializing in training soldiers who will be able to lead on the front lines in various military engagements.

Ranger School trains Army Rangers who want to advance to leadership positions within the Army Ranger Regiment.

BENNING PHASE

During the Benning Phase of Ranger School, students will build their skills in combat, physical fitness, and mental endurance. The training students receive prepares them to maintain their equipment, keep their fellow soldiers alive during combat, and survive the most difficult of situations themselves. Rangers must be prepared to perform effectively in the worst of circumstances and the harshest of environments.

The Benning Phase of Ranger School is itself split into two phases. The first phase is called the Ranger Assessment Phase (RAP). Ranger students must complete what is called the Ranger Physical Fitness Test, which requires forty-nine pushups, fifty-nine sit-ups, and six chin-ups. In addition, Rangers must complete a five-mile run in less than forty minutes.

The week-long Ranger Assessment Phase also includes the Combat Water Survival Assessment; a twelve-mile foot march; and of a three-mile run, immediately followed by completion of the Malvesti obstacle course, all in full combat gear while carrying a weapon. This first part of Benning Phase also includes a refresher course on Airborne training, including jumps from aircraft.

The second part of Benning Phase takes place at Camp Darby, named for William Darby, trainer of the First, Third, and Fourth Ranger Battalions during World War II. This phase of training is centered around patrolling procedures and larger-scale combat operations alongside soldiers other than the RAP. In addition, Ranger students must complete a three-day platoon field-training exercise (FTX).

During the course of this second part of Benning Phase, students complete the Darby Queen Obstacle Course and receive instruction on mission planning and patrol techniques. They also conduct battle drills, including reconnaissance and ambush-training exercises.

In the three-day FTX, students apply their knowledge of mission planning, and combat techniques to organize and execute a successful operation. Rangers also build their ability to work with and lead others during these operations, many of which are entirely led by students. Once students have completed all the requirements of this second part of Benning Phase, they are prepared for the Mountain Phase of Ranger School.

The Fourth Ranger Training Battalion (RTB) has the job of training students in the Benning phase of Ranger School. The Benning phase, also called the "crawl" phase (as in "crawl, walk, run"), is designed to build and improve the tactical skills, physical ability, mental endurance, and confidence that all soldiers in the U.S. Army—and Rangers in particular—must possess.

MOUNTAIN PHASE

The Mountain Phase of Ranger School prepares Ranger students for operations in mountainous environments through instruction on mountaineering techniques. Students continue to hone their mission planning and execution skills, as well as their leadership and teamwork abilities. They must face the hardships of mountainous terrain, hunger, extreme weather, and physical fatigue, all while maintaining combat effectiveness. In addition to building their combat expertise during the Mountain Phase of training, students also must undergo four days of training in mountaineering. This training is completed in two phases, Lower first, followed by Upper. In the Lower part of mountaineering training, Ranger students learn about tying knots, managing rope during climbing, and the basics of rappelling. During the Upper part of training, Ranger students train in the field, carrying out combat patrols that require them to apply their mountaineering knowledge learned in Lower part of training.

During the Mountain Phase of Ranger School, students conduct combat missions against a mock enemy threat. They carry out patrol missions during the day and at night over the course of both four- and five-day field-training exercises. These operations include movement across mountainous terrain, ambushing enemy vehicles, and conducting raid missions. Rangers must exhibit the **stamina** it takes to be an Army Ranger during this operation, as they may be called upon at any time to lead students who are physically and mentally drained, pushed to their limits.

The Fifth Ranger Training Battalion trains Ranger students during the Mountain Phase of Ranger School. They are responsible for preparing students to carry out missions and combat operations on mountainous terrain as individuals and with other soldiers.

UNDERSTAND THE FULL MEANING

stamina: The ability to maintain physical performance over a long period of time.

Rangers negotiating the Darby Queen obstacle course at Camp Darby, in Fort Benning, Georgia.

Soldiers receiving instructions on rappelling during the Mountain Phase of Army Ranger School.

FLORIDA PHASE

The third and final phase of training at Ranger School, Florida Phase, is conducted at Camp James E. Rudder, Eglin Air Force Base, Florida. During this phase, Ranger students continue to improve their combat skills. All Rangers must be prepared to face extraordinary physical and mental stress during their service in the Seventy-Fifth Ranger Regiment. To achieve the level of combat expertise, physical ability, and mental toughness that Rangers need, students train in the swamps of Florida, participating in realistic (though **simulated**) combat exercises. Students learn to further apply their knowledge of air assaults, patrol operations, small-boat transport, and on-foot combat.

The Sixth Ranger Training Battalion is responsible for training and instructing students in their final phase of Ranger School. They provide students with the most realistic combat training possible, so that they are absolutely prepared to lead the way in any combat scenario. The instructors in the Sixth RTB also review students' performance in combat exercises, giving them advice on how to improve if need be. The Sixth RTB's Ranger Support Element (RSE) assists in training students in realistic battle situations by engaging students in simulated combat when they are least expecting attack, pushing them to improve their decision-making skills under pressure.

UNDERSTAND THE FULL MEANING

simulated: A situation that is created for training purposes that closely resembles real-life conditions.

CHAPTER 4

Modern Missions

I n the modern era, the Rangers have been called upon once again the to lead the way, this time in the wars in Afghanistan and Iraq. Since the terrorist attacks of September 11, 2001,the Rangers have been deployed in both Operation Enduring Freedom and Iraqi Freedom. For the first time in its history, the Seventy-Fifth Ranger Regiment is serving in multiple armed conflicts, in different parts of the world, deploying from different parts of the United States simultaneously. In addition, the Seventy-Fifth Ranger Regiment is also one of a few select U.S. military units to be deployed continually since the beginning of Operation Enduring Freedom in Afghanistan in 2001. Every single Ranger serving today has or will be deployed overseas. In both Operation Enduring Freedom and Iraqi Freedom, Rang-

ers have carried out a wide variety of missions, including raid, reconnaissance, and rescue work.

While conducting missions abroad, the Seventy-Fifth Ranger Regiment also continues to remain vigilant through

During counter IED training, an Airborne Ranger teaches U.S. Marines about the types of improvised explosive devices (IEDs) usually found in Afghanistan during Operation Enduring Freedom.

training both in the United States and overseas. The Rangers must be ready for "no-notice" deployment to any part of the world. Within hours, a Ranger battalion can have its boots on the ground anywhere on the face of the Earth. The next generation of Rangers is also continually being brought through the rigorous training of the Seventy-Fifth Regiment, so that they too are prepared for deployment at any time.

FIRST BATTALION

In December 2001, a few months after September 11, Rangers from the First Battalion's Headquarters Company and A Company deployed to Afghanistan as part of Operation Enduring Freedom. The following year, the First Battalion deployed to Afghanistan in full, supporting the ongoing war against terrorist networks operating in the country (including elements of Al Qaida, perpetrators of the September 11 terrorist attacks on New York and Pentagon in Washington, D.C.), as well as the Taliban regime that harbors them.

In 2003, the First Battalion was deployed to Iraq to assist other American military forces in Operation Iraqi Freedom. In missions spanning the entire country, the First Battalion distinguished itself time and time again as the United States' top soldiers. Their missions included the rescue of American prisoners and a variety of combat missions.

At the end of that year, the battalion split its forces, deploying Rangers to both Iraq and Afghanistan. Since that time, Rangers from the First Battalion have served in both wars, working tirelessly to kill or capture terrorist networks

Rangers may parachute into an area during a mission, or they may descend from a low-flying helicopter like this MH-47 Chinook.

seeking to harm the United States and its allies around the globe.

SECOND BATTALION

In March of 2002, the Second Battalion deployed to Afghanistan to assist in Operation Enduring Freedom. During that time, the Battalion conducted raid, ambush, and air-assault missions against enemy forces. Later that year, in December, elements of the Second Battalion were deployed to Afghanistan for a second time to continue the mission of American forces in the region.

In February 2003, the Rangers of the Second Battalion not already serving in the war in Afghanistan deployed as part of Operation Iraqi Freedom. The Second Battalion was the first American military unit to reach Baghdad, Iraq's capital, and erect a base of operations in the city. In late 2003, the Second Battalion was sent to Afghanistan to aid once more in the fight against terrorist networks and their supporters. Rangers conducted missions into the most dangerous and difficult to navigate areas of the country, hunting down the enemy, no matter his location. At altitudes of more than 9,000 feet (2.7 km) in the mountains of Afghanistan, Rangers carried out raids on key enemy targets in order to support U.S. objectives. Throughout 2004, the Second Battalion was split between the wars in Iraq and Afghanistan, and to this day, the significant majority of Ranger missions have been conducted in one of these two conflicts.

THIRD BATTALION

During the night of October 19, 2001, a little more than a month after the events of September 11, parts of the Third Battalion conducted a low-altitude parachute drop into Afghanistan. Their objective was to capture an airfield in the southwest of the country that held vital strategic information, code-named Objective Rhino. This initial airfield assault was one of the first missions of Operation Enduring Freedom. In a later airfield raid mission, Rangers from the

U.S. Army Special Forces are active in parts of the world other than Iraq and Afghanistan—these soldiers are helping a wounded soldier in the Philippines.

Third Battalion captured a desert landing strip in order to assist a Special Operations mission.

In March of 2003, the early days of Operation Iraqi Freedom, the Third Battalion was the first U.S. military unit to conduct an airborne assault in Iraq. Rangers from the Third Battalion were to seize Objective Serpent, the Iraqi capitol of Baghdad. In the following weeks, the Third Battalion also parachuted onto the H2 Airfield in the West of Iraq, successfully assaulting their target. On the 31st of March, Rangers from the Third Battalion gained ground in the battle for the Hadithah Dam facility, fighting the Iraqi Republican Guard over the course of a week in order to secure the objective.

REGIMENTAL SPECIAL TROOPS BATTALION (RSTB)

War has changed dramatically in recent years, as the flow of information within the military takes on greater and greater importance. In light of the changing nature of war, as well as the prolonged deployment of Ranger Battalions serving in Afghanistan and Iraq, the Rangers needed additional technological and communications assistance in the field. On July 17, 2006, the Regimental Special Troops Battalion (RSTB) was activated. The RSTB is responsible for intelligence, reconnaissance, maintenance, and force—**sustain-**

UNDERSTAND THE FULL MEANING

sustainment: The supplying of troops with all things necessary for their success in the field.

ment missions that were once conducted by small groups from the Seventy-Fifth Ranger Regiment headquarters attached to each Ranger battalion. The creation of the RSTB allows the three main Ranger Battalions to focus on combat missions while they are sustained and informed by another battalion, affording the Rangers even greater flexibility. At a time when the Rangers have been deployed continuously for almost a decade, the RTSB also enables long-term overseas commitments.

RANGER OPERATIONS

Today's Rangers are involved in a variety of combat missions in both the war in Afghanistan and the war in Iraq. Here are a few examples of the types of operations Rangers conduct in support of American strategic goals.

DIRECT ACTION

The majority of the missions Rangers conduct can be considered direct-action operations. They involve quickly getting into an area, often occupied by the enemy, and completing objectives efficiently. These actions are often surprise attacks on enemy targets or troops. The methods Rangers use to reach their objectives, and the types of missions they carry out once they arrive, can vary depending on the goals of the action.

Rangers are all trained Airborne School graduates, and every Ranger has the skills and knowledge to conduct parachute jumps in order to get to his objective during a mission.

U.S. Army rangers assigned to the 6th Ranger Training Battalion prepare to board a U.S. Air Force C-130 Hercules aircraft.

Rangers may also use other methods to reach an objective or target, including boats or helicopters. Rangers use what are called fast lines (ropes that allow a soldier to quickly descend from an air vehicle) in order to drop from low-flying helicopters.

As a unit, the Army Rangers are also extraordinarily flexible. They are able to move from what is considered a special operation to a more **conventional** one. If the Rangers are ordered to capture an enemy airfield (a common mission for the Rangers), for instance, they will likely parachute into the area, remove any threats, take the airfield, and then signal that their initial mission is completed successfully. When additional U.S. or coalition forces enter the area, Rangers are able to connect with them and move forward as part of a larger, conventional military force.

These types of missions are called direct-action operations. They are almost always dangerous and involve armed combat.

RECONNAISSANCE

Reconnaissance, called recon for short, is a key part of the responsibilities of the Army Rangers. The Rangers are extremely qualified for these types of operations, and have been since the time of their fighting in the Revolutionary War, and on through their jungle patrols in Vietnam. Though all Rangers are taught how to per-

UNDERSTAND THE FULL MEANING

conventional: Refers to military activity that is most usual and common, rather than the operations of Special Forces.

form recon and conduct missions in order to gather intelligence, a select few are trained specifically in scouting and reconnaissance work. These Rangers serve as part of the Regimental Reconnaissance Detachment (RRD).

Army Rangers from the 1st Battalion, 75th Ranger Regiment fly into a city on a MH-6 Little Bird helicopter before dismounting onto a rooftop during a training exercise. These exercises prepare Rangers for real-life deployment into urban areas.

Started in 1984, the RRD is made up of three teams of four men each. These scouts are experienced and highly trained, able to survive for almost a week behind enemy lines without being detected or communicating with their superiors or fellow Rangers. The RRD consists of just twelve Rangers for the entire Seventy-Fifth Regiment, one team of four for each Ranger Battalion. RRD Rangers are responsible for confirming the truth of intelligence (or proving it is poor intelligence) by monitoring the enemy through use of electronic surveillance equipment and human observation. These Rangers must report the movement of enemy troops to their superiors and assess targets before helping to coordinate attacks on them. In some cases, the RRD has been involved in direct-action missions, in which they are part of a raid or assault team of other Rangers, but the RRD Rangers are usually ordered to simply move in and out of enemy territory without being detected.

RESCUE

The Rangers are uniquely qualified for many rescue missions, due to their level of expertise. Rescue missions are usually equal parts reconnaissance and direct action. Rangers have to discover the location of prisoners or missing soldiers by confirming intelligence that may point them in the right direction. This may include gathering information from intelligence sources or recon missions. Once the location of the target of the rescue mission is clear, Rangers often must fight to their objective and then fight to escape enemy territory. Experts at getting in and getting out of any situation quickly and without detection, Rangers are the ideal soldiers to take on dangerous rescue missions.

AFGHAN COMMANDOS: INSPIRED BY U.S. ARMY RANGERS

One of the most important parts of both the wars in Iraq and Afghanistan is training local forces, so that they may take over the combat and peacekeeping operations for which the U.S. military has been responsible. As President George W. Bush once said, "As they stand up, we'll stand down." President Barack Obama also committed more troops to Afghanistan in 2010, increasing the significance of the role local forces have in securing the country.

The Afghan National Army (ANA) also has its own commando forces, based partially on the U.S. Army Rangers. Called Commando Kandaks (Battalions), the Afghan Special Forces undergo training similar to that of the Army Rangers, with emphasis on realistic combat scenarios during instruction. Once trained, Afghan commandos travel with American Special Forces personnel in order to get a field view of the types of operations in which they will need to become experts. This partnering phase of training has become a vital component of training local forces to carry out dangerous and combat-heavy missions.

The Afghan commandos also receive high-quality military equipment, including night-vision goggles, and weapons

An Afghan National Army (ANA) commando takes up a defensive position next to a poppy field in Afghanistan.

including M-4 carbines, M-240 machine guns, and M-249 squad automatic weapons. They are given communications equipment, uniforms, and gear for use in the field (such as portable cookware for making hot meals). The majority of the items provided to Afghan commandos are the same as those used by the U.S. Army Rangers.

In the Summer of 2007, the First Commando Kandak graduated from training ready to serve in the ANA as part of coalition forces in Afghanistan. The first of six kandaks to be trained by the U.S. Military before the ANA began training its own commandos, the First Commando Kandak was a sign of the growing emphasis on well-trained, elite fighting forces coming up from local populations in the continued efforts of the military in Afghanistan and in Iraq, where local soldiers have made the difference time and time again.

The commander of the First Commando Kandak, Lieutenant Colonel Mohammad Farid Ahmadi, has said that his unit working out supply-related and **logistical** issues will make training and preparation an easier process for the next kandak. The influence of the Army Rangers and their excellent reputation within the military are reflected in the service of Afghanistan's First Commando Kandak.

UNDERSTAND THE FULL MEANING

logistical: Having to do with the movement of resources to supply military troops.

CHAPTER 5
Weapons and Gear

The modern Army Rangers are equipped with the best weapons and gear that the U.S. Army can provide. The Rangers are armed with the finest in military equipment so that they are always capable of effective combat. The tools Rangers use to complete their missions in service of the United States are not simple to use. They require the utmost in training and education. With the right equipment, weapons, and knowledge about how to use both to the maximum effect, the Army Rangers are able to tackle any mission at any time.

TODAY'S WEAPONS

The Army Rangers must be able to deliver the firepower needed to subdue enemy forces in the missions they conduct in the wars in Iraq and Afghanistan. The weapons Rangers

A U.S. Army soldier from B/Company, 1st Battalion, 75th Ranger Regiment carries a 5.56mm Colt M4 carbine during training at Fort Stewart, Georgia.

use are the deadly tools of their trade. They must understand how to use and maintain them properly in order for them to remain effective. Here are a few examples of weapons used by today's U.S. Army Rangers.

M-4

The Army first used the M-4 assault rifle in 1997. Today, the M-4 is used by some of the Army's finest units, including the 82nd Airborne Division and the Rangers. The M-4 continues the legacy of the M-16, the Army's standard assault rifle for many years, and before that the M-1 Carbine (used by the Rangers in World War II and the Korean War).

The rifle has a shorter barrel than many other similar weapons, and a stock that can be collapsed, making it excellent for close-quarters firing, where soldiers will need a light weapon for quick movement. The M-4 can also be equipped with an infrared sight, allowing increased accuracy. In addition, the M-4 can be outfitted with a M-203 40mm grenade launcher, giving infantry even greater firepower.

M249 SAW (SQUAD AUTOMATIC WEAPON)

Replacing the older M-60 machine gun, the M-249 SAW first saw use in the U.S. Army in 1987. Though initial models of this weapon were considered to be too problematic to use, the current version of the M-249 is a staple of the U.S. Army's arsenal.

The M-249 fires at a rate of 750 5.56mm rounds per minute. The weapon is belt fed, meaning that its ammunition is held on a belt located in a box on the underside of the gun. Some components of the M-249 are made of plastic, including the pistol grip, cutting down the overall weight of the weapon. The gun is light enough to be carried and fired by one soldier, even when carrying two hundred rounds in its ammunition box.

In a number of trials on the M-249, the U.S. Army concluded that the weapon has a far lower failure rate than similar weapons, making it an even more valuable part of America's arsenal.

Members of the 75th Rangers (Airborne), Fort Benning, Georgia, armed with M16 rifles with M203 grenade launcher (kneeling) and M249 SAW light machine guns (prone position), perform weapons training.

M-240

The U.S. Army began using the M-240 machine gun in 1997. The M-240 replaced the older machine guns in use at that time. The weapon fires 7.62 mm bullets. It is estimated that the M-240 can fire 26,000 bullets (on average) before failing to fire a single time. The M-240 is used around the world by many different military organizations. This increases the value of the M-240, rather than diminishing it, especially considering its use today in wars fought by coalitions of nations, rather than the United States acting alone. The M-240 weighs just over twenty-seven pounds (12 kg).

The weapon can also be configured in a variety of ways, making it easier to use in many different scenarios. For example, in the event of a helicopter crash, the M-240d that is mounted inside the helicopter can easily be modified using pieces (such as the butt and bipod) of the M-240b, allowing survivors of the crash to carry the weapon with them for defense.

RANGERS' EQUIPMENT

The equipment Rangers use is vital to their conducting combat missions successfully. They are experts in using a variety of technologies, many that have been in use for years and many that are brand new, in order to effectively support U.S. operations around the world. Here are a few examples of key items of Ranger equipment.

ADVANCED TACTICAL PARACHUTE SYSTEM

The weight of the gear carried by Rangers can become a burden, but much of it is vital to their survival in combat. Recently, the Army commissioned a redesign of the parachute system it has been using for years, specifically so that the parachute could hold 400 pounds (181 kg), the estimate of how much soldiers might weigh while wearing the equip-

Army Rangers from the 1st Battalion, 75th Ranger Regiment conduct an urban assault on a mock city during a training exercise at Fort Bragg, North Carolina.

ment they need for a jump. The new parachute system is called the T-11 Advanced Tactical Parachute System. The Seventy-Fifth Ranger Regiment was the first unit in the Army to use the T-11, an upgrade of the T-10 system.

The T-10 system had a faster rate of descent for the average soldier than the T-11, one benefit of the new design. Rangers weighing drop at a rate of about 19 feet (6 m) per second with the new T-11, while the jumpers using the T-10 dropped at a rate of 22 feet (7 m) per second. This is a marked improvement for the Rangers using these parachute systems, particularly since a slower fall means less impact when soldiers land after a jump. The T-11 also prevents jumpers from swinging from side to side after opening their chute. Rangers jumping with the T-11 will experience a less violent parachute opening, due to what is called lower opening shock rate, something that caused issues with the T-10 system.

NIGHT-VISION GOGGLES

Due to the number of nighttime operations the Army Rangers conduct, they must be able to see in the dark just as well as they would be able to during the day. Called NVDs (Night Vision Devices), night-vision goggles give Rangers the edge when carrying out night raids or rescue missions. Rather than relying on bringing light with them (flashlights, for instance), Rangers use night-vision goggles that enhance existing environmental light, including **spectrum** not vis-

UNDERSTAND THE FULL MEANING

spectrum: Referring to a range of light intensity based on wavelength of light rays.

ible to the human eye, allowing Rangers to remain unseen by enemy forces, even as they are able to see clearly in the darkest of situations.

One model of night-vision goggles used by the U.S. Military, including the Army Rangers, is the PVS-14 Monocular

Night vision goggles render the world green, but allow Rangers to perform missions under the cover of darkness without needing to carry flashlights.

Night-Vision Device. This set of goggles has a single scope as opposed to two, monocular rather than binocular. These goggles carry with them a device called an illuminator that fires a beam of light that the human eye cannot see, allowing a Ranger wearing the PVS-14 to see more clearly without giving away his presence to the enemy. When a soldier uses the PVS-14, he views the environment on a screen inside the device. The device can also be worn underneath a Ranger's helmet. Like many consumer electronic products, the PVS-14 system runs on two AA batteries.

FLAK VEST

Flak vests protect soldiers against being struck by shrapnel from an explosion, some types of gunfire, and a variety of other attacks with lethal potential. Flak vests, worn by all Rangers, are made of a material called Kevlar®. Kevlar is in the bulletproof vests that police wear, as well.

In 2002, the Army and Marine Corps started using flak vests that were 35 percent lighter than the previously used version of the same armor. Called the Interceptor, the new vests have guards for solders' necks and groins that can be removed when increased mobility is needed. These vests can stop a round from a 9mm pistol and protect a soldier from being hit in the chest or torso by shrapnel. In addition, further protective plating can be added to the vest, allowing it to stop the bullets from some types of rifles.

The lighter weight of the Interceptor body armor, as well as its interchangeable parts, make it the best protection from gunfire, mines, grenades, mortars, and other poten-

These soldiers in Afghanistan are adjusting their flak vests, which will help protect them from shrapnel and gunfire.

tially lethal attack. The Army Rangers use this type of armor in many different kinds of operations and training exercises.

Equipment like this is essential to the Rangers. But it is their courage and dedication that makes them the elite force they are.

FIND OUT MORE ON THE INTERNET

Army Recruiting www.goarmy.com

Department of Defense www.defense.gov

Seventy-Fifth Ranger Regiment www.benning.army.mil/75thranger/

U.S. Army www.army.mil

U.S Army Airborne School www.benning.army.mil/airborne/airborne/

U.S. Army Fort Jackson (Basic Combat Training)
www.jackson.army.mil/

U.S. Army Special Operations Command (SOC) www.soc.mil

The websites listed on this page were active at the time of publication. The publisher is not responsible for websites that have changed their address or discontinued operation since the date of publication. The publisher will review and update the websites upon each reprint.

FURTHER READING

Barber, Brace, E. *No Excuse Leadership: Lessons from the U.S. Army's Elite Rangers*. Hoboken, N.J.: Wiley, 2004.

Bahmanyar, Mir. *Shadow Warriors: A History of the U.S. Army Rangers*. Oxford, UK: Osprey Publishing, 2006.

Black, Robert W. *Rangers in World War II*. New York: Presidio Press, 2002.

Bohrer, David. *America's Special Forces: Seals, Green Berets, Rangers, USAF Special Ops, Marine Force Recon*. St. Paul, Minn.: Zenith Press, 2002.

Bryant, Russ. *To Be a U.S. Army Ranger.* St. Paul, Minn.: MBI Publishing Company, 2003.

Bryant, Russ. *Weapons of the U.S. Army Rangers*. St. Paul, Minn.: Zenith Press, 2005.

Lock, J. D. *Rangers in Combat: A Legacy of Valor*. Tucson, Ariz.: Wheatmark, 2007.

Sizer, Mona D. *The Glory Guys: The Story of the U.S. Army Rangers*. Lanham, Md.: Taylor Trade Publishing, 2010.

U.S. Department of Defense. *United States Army Ranger Handbook*. New York: Skyhorse Publishing, 2007.

BIBILIOGRAPHY

About.com, "United States Military Weapons of War," usmilitary.about.com/od/armyweapons/l/aainfantry1.htm (3 June 2010).

Graham, Ian, "General sees positives in Afghan army training," www.army.mil/-news/2010/02/22/34770-general-sees-positives-in-afghan-army-training/ (1 June 2010).

How Stuff Works, "How the Army Rangers Work,"science.howstuffworks.com/army-ranger.htm (2 June 2010).

How Stuff Works, "How the U.S. Army Works," science.howstuffworks.com/army.htm (2 June 2010).

United States Army, www.army.mil/info/organization/jackson/, (1 June 2010).

United States Army, "Best Ranger Competition," www.army.mil/ranger/2010/about.html (1 June 2010).

United States Army, "75th Ranger Regiment," www.goarmy.com/ranger/index.jsp (2 June 2010).

United States Army, "Soldier Life," www.goarmy.com/life/basic/index.jsp (2 June 2010).

USASOC, "75th Ranger Regiment," www.soc.mil/75thrr/75thrrfs.html (3 June 2010).

Votroubek, David, "New Gear for Afghan Commandos," www.almc.army.mil/alog/issues/JulAug08/newgear_afghan.html (1 June 2010).

Wired.com, "New Chute Means 'Softer' Landing for Paratroopers," www.wired.com/dangerroom/2009/08/new-chute-means-softer-landing-for-paratroopers/ (3 June 2010).

INDEX

PICTURE CREDITS

ABOUT THE AUTHORS

Gabrielle Vanderhoof is a former competitive figure skater. She now works in publishing and public relations. This is her first time writing for Mason Crest.

CF Earl is a writer living and working in Binghamton, New York. Earl writes mostly on social and historical topics, including health, the military, and finances, among other topics. An avid student of the world around him, and particularly fascinated with almost any current issue, CF Earl hopes to continue to write for books, websites, and other publications for as long as he is able.

ABOUT THE CONSULTANT

Colonel John Carney, Jr. is USAF-Retired, President and the CEO of the Special Operations Warrior Foundation.